Andrew Brodie

Improving
Spelling

for ages 8–9

A & C Black • London

Improving Spelling for Ages 8–9 features 42 sets of words, chosen to complement and extend the programme of activities that pupils will have experienced through 'Letters and Sounds'. The pupils will not need to work slavishly through the lists of words. However, if the lists are used on a regular basis as the focus for a short activity, they will help to provide a structured approach to improving pupils' skills in both reading and spelling.

Most pupils enjoy the security of following a repeated pattern in their work. Accordingly, each set of words is presented in two styles of sheet with which the pupils will soon become familiar:

SHEET A

Sheet A features the 10 focus words to encourage the children to:

Look, listen and learn

This sheet can be:
- Displayed on the whiteboard for discussion.
- Copied on to card and cut up to make matching cards.
- Displayed on the wall as 'Words of the Week'.

Encouraging the children to 'sound-talk' the words. For example, the word pick can be sound-talked 'p-i-c-k' but be careful not to add 'uh' to sounds, i.e. say 'p' not 'puh'!

SHEET B

Sheet B provides practice activities:

Look and write
Encourages the children to look carefully at the structure of each word.

Listen and write
Encourages the children to listen carefully to the phonemes within each word, to help them to segment the word for spelling.

This sheet can be:
- Displayed on the whiteboard for discussion.
- Photocopied as individual activity sheets.
- Cut in half to make two separate activity sheets.

The book also features five sheets that can be copied and enlarged to make Spelling Strategy Posters, as recommended in 'Letters and Sounds'. You can use these as a focus for discussing strategies that pupils can employ when learning new spellings.

CONTENTS

Pupil record sheet
Spelling Strategy poster: Syllables
Spelling Strategy poster: Base words
Spelling Strategy poster: Analogy
Spelling Strategy poster: Mnemonics
Spelling poster: Strategies

Set 1 place places badge badges river rivers hospital hospitals college colleges
Set 2 match matches catch catches bush bushes switch switches dish dishes
Set 3 pony ponies lady ladies hobby hobbies ferry ferries strawberry strawberries
Set 4 mouse mice person people tooth teeth woman women half halves
Set 5 running hopping hoping coming catching trying planting flowering carrying reaching
Set 6 hopped hoped laughed shaped searched reached greeted coated waited striped
Set 7 kettle bottle middle giggle wriggle little puddle table double noble
Set 8 bigger biggest larger largest narrower narrowest wider widest thinner thinnest
Set 9 flop floppy floppier floppiest happier happiest funnier funniest sun run
Set 10 happily funnily warmly coldly repeat repeated repeatedly real really usual
Set 11 wonderful beauty beautiful careful hopeful useful wonderfully beautifully carefully usefully
Set 12 careless hopeless meaningless helpless useless carelessly hopelessly uselessly painless harmless
Set 13 it's we'll we've we're isn't can't haven't doesn't won't they're
Set 14 cat's cats' boy's boys' girl's girls' child's children's woman's women's
Set 15 right fright bright brighter brighten frighten frightening high height flight
Set 16 cough tough enough ought bought though through thought bough brought
Set 17 laugh laughing laughed daughter teach teacher taught catch catching caught
Set 18 wallet warm wall wander want watch waste water wave wax
Set 19 wobble woke woman women wonder won't wool word worn worry
Set 20 boss floss passage possible impossible possibility impossibility possibilities guess guessing
Set 21 page cage stage teenager teenaged passage carriage marriage bridge fridge
Set 22 about found ground amount couch crouch ouch loud cloud proud
Set 23 blot plot knot squat swat what yacht dotted spot spotted
Set 24 haul autumn taught caught aunt auntie aunty cause because sausage
Set 25 double trouble four fourteen forty pour young younger youngest journey
Set 26 motorway birthday underwater waterproof overcrowded overhead overload overnight undercover underground
Set 27 terrible horrible terribly horribly responsible responsibly reversible visible invisible edible
Set 28 laughable break broke broken breakable value valuable enjoy enjoyable enjoyment
Set 29 station nation national pollute polluted pollution information education relation educational
Set 30 addition subtract subtraction multiply multiplication divide division calculate calculation calculating
Set 31 revision explosion confuse confused confusion decision invasion tension extension mansion
Set 32 infect infection infectious delicious vicious ambition ambitious reflect reflected reflection
Set 33 quick quicker quickly ticket cricket cricketer tickle trickle prickle prickly
Set 34 swim swimming swimmer swam trim trimming trimmer trimmed glimmer skim
Set 35 miscalculate mislead nonsense non-fiction non-iron impossible exchange inactive co-star anticlockwise
Set 36 bicycle recalculate tricycle abnormal rearrange prearrange precast prejudge preschool preview
Set 37 unusual unusually untrue unhappy unhappily unknown unless unlikely unlocked unlucky
Set 38 disinfect disobey disobeyed disobedient disqualify deforest decode debug deflate defrost
Set 39 interactive interlocking interior exterior international internet submarine subtitle subtract suburbs
Set 40 happiness carelessness silliness craziness madness friendship hardship spaceship membership premiership
Set 41 childhood neighbourhood expense expensive compete competitive attract attractive active activity
Set 42 metre centimetre millimetre kilometre litre millilitre centilitre gram milligram kilogram

Assessments

You could record your pupils' progress using the 'traffic light' system: red for not yet secure, orange for secure, green for competent.

Name																							
Set 1																							
Set 2																							
Set 3																							
Set 4																							
Set 5																							
Set 6																							
Set 7																							
Set 8																							
Set 9																							
Set 10																							
Set 11																							
Set 12																							
Set 13																							
Set 14																							
Set 15																							
Set 16																							
Set 17																							
Set 18																							
Set 19																							
Set 20																							
Set 21																							
Set 22																							
Set 23																							
Set 24																							
Set 25																							
Set 26																							
Set 27																							
Set 28																							
Set 29																							
Set 30																							
Set 31																							
Set 32																							
Set 33																							
Set 34																							
Set 35																							
Set 36																							
Set 37																							
Set 38																							
Set 39																							
Set 40																							
Set 41																							
Set 42																							

To help me with spelling I can use . . .

Syllables

by breaking words into chunks.

Look:

multiply

mul-ti-ply

To help me with spelling I can use . . .

Base words

Some words are based on other words.

Look:

swimming

swim

The base word is **swim**.

To add the ing ending we need to double the m.

Andrew Brodie: Improving Spelling for Ages 8–9 © A&C Black, Bloomsbury Publishing 2011

To help me with spelling
I can use . . .

Similar words

Some words are similar
to other words.

Look:

horrible

terrible

Both words have ible.

To help me with spelling
I can use . . .

Mnemonics

If I'm really stuck I can make up a phrase or sentence to help me remember.

Look:

people

people **e**at **o**ther **p**eople's **l**unches **e**asily

If I am stuck on spelling a word I can . . .

1 use **phonics** to help me.

2 try breaking a big word into **syllables**.

3 think about whether it's made from a **base word**.

4 think about **similar words**.

5 **look** for the word.

6 **ask** for help.

7 use **mnemonics** to learn the word.

Look, listen and learn

place	places
badge	badges
river	rivers
hospital	hospitals
college	colleges

Look and write

place

places

badge

badges

river

rivers

hospital

hospitals

college

colleges

Listen and write

There are some lovely _____ by the _____.

_____

The _____ is next to the _____.

_____

The Amazon and the Nile are the longest _____ in the world.

_____

The staff in _____ wear name _____.

_____

Look, listen and learn

match	matches
catch	catches
bush	bushes
switch	switches
dish	dishes

Teacher's notes

Sheet A, Look, listen and learn: Use the words on this page as a focus for discussing phonic patterns and word structures. Encourage the pupils to notice the sound that the suffix 'es' represents. What's special about the words? Do the children notice that the words are arranged in pairs? What's special about the pairs? Do the children notice that the words have a different number of syllables once the suffix 'es' is added? Ask pairs or small groups of children to create two spoken sentences for the different pairs of words.

Sheet B, Look and write: Encourage the children to look closely at the words and to practise writing them.

Sheet B, Listen and write: Dictate each sentence below to the children, emphasising the target words. Encourage the children to copy each sentence in full on the line underneath it. You could extend the activity by asking the children to make up their own sentence using one or more of the target words.

My socks don't match because they are different colours.   We had two football matches last week.
I tried to catch the ball before it went into the bushes.   How many light switches are there in this room?

Look and write

match	matches
catch	catches
bush	bushes
switch	switches
dish	dishes

Listen and write

My socks don't _____ because they are different colours.

_____

We had two football _____ last week.

_____

I tried to _____ the ball before it went into the _____ .

_____

How many light _____ are there in this room?

_____

Look, listen and learn

pony	ponies
lady	ladies
hobby	hobbies
ferry	ferries
strawberry	strawberries

Teacher's notes

Sheet A, Look, listen and learn: Use the words on this page as a focus for discussing phonic patterns and word structures. Encourage the pupils to notice that the 'y' on the base word is removed and replaced with a letter 'i' when the suffix 'es' is added to make the word become plural. Ask pairs or small groups of children to create two spoken sentences for the different pairs of words.

Sheet B, Look and write: Encourage the children to look closely at the words and to practise writing them.

Sheet B, Listen and write: Dictate each sentence below to the children, emphasising the target words. Encourage the children to copy each sentence in full on the line underneath it. You could extend the activity by asking the children to make up their own sentence using one or more of the target words.

The grey pony is smaller than the other ponies.   Three young ladies were picking strawberries.
Some people have lots of hobbies.   Two ferries came into the harbour.

Look and write

pony

ponies

lady

ladies

hobby

hobbies

ferry

ferries

strawberry

strawberries

Listen and write

The grey _____ is smaller than the other _____ .

_____

Three young _____ were picking _____ .

_____

Some people have lots of _____ .

_____

Two _____ came into the harbour.

_____

Look, listen and learn

mouse	mice
person	people
tooth	teeth
woman	women
half	halves

Teacher's notes

Sheet A, Look, listen and learn: Use the words on this page as a focus for discussing phonic patterns and word structures. Encourage the pupils to notice that all of the singular words have unusual plural forms. Talk about the sounds in the words – for example, what sound does the grapheme o make in the word 'woman' and what sound does it make in the word 'women'? Ask pairs or small groups of children to create two spoken sentences for the different pairs of words.

Sheet B, Look and write: Encourage the children to look closely at the words and to practise writing them.

Sheet B, Listen and write: Dictate each sentence below to the children, emphasising the target words. Encourage the children to copy each sentence in full on the line underneath it. Point out the use of an apostrophe in the third sentence to show possession – the children should learn that the apostrophe is used after the 'owner', ie the gymnastics belong to the women so the apostrophe appears after the word 'women'. You could extend the activity by asking the children to make up their own sentence using one or more of the target words.

The white mouse is smaller than the two other mice.   Most people take good care of their teeth.

Women's gymnastics is a very popular sport.   The game was in two halves and the second half was better than the first.

Look and write

mouse

mice

person

people

tooth

teeth

woman

women

half

halves

Listen and write

The white _____ is smaller than the two other _____ .

Most _____ take good care of their _____ .

_____ gymnastics is a very popular sport.

The game was in two _____ and the second _____ was better than the first.

Look, listen and learn

running	hopping
hoping	coming
catching	trying
planting	flowering
carrying	reaching

Sheet A, Look, listen and learn: Use the words on this page as a focus for discussing phonic patterns and word structures. Encourage the pupils to observe how the suffix 'ing' is added to each of the base words: for example, do they notice that the final consonant of the word 'hop' is doubled and the final 'e' of the word 'hope' is removed? Ask pairs or small groups of children to create two spoken sentences for the different pairs of words.

Sheet B, Look and write: Encourage the children to look closely at the words and to practise writing them.

Sheet B, Listen and write: Dictate each sentence below to the children, emphasising the target words. Encourage the children to copy each sentence in full on the line underneath it. You could extend the activity by asking the children to make up their own sentence using one or more of the target words.

I like running and hopping. Sometimes I am not good at catching the ball even though I am trying very hard.
The lavender plants are flowering early this year. I was hoping to find some chocolate when I was reaching up to the top shelf.

Look and write

running

hopping

hoping

coming

catching

trying

planting

flowering

carrying

reaching

Listen and write

I like _____ and _____ .

_____

Sometimes I am not good at _____ the ball even though I am

_____ very hard.

_____

The lavender plants are _____ early this year.

_____

I was _____ to find some chocolate when I was _____ up

to the top shelf.

_____

Look, listen and learn

hopped	hoped
laughed	shaped
searched	reached
greeted	coated
waited	striped

Teacher's notes

Sheet A, Look, listen and learn: Use the words on this page as a focus for discussing phonic patterns and word structures. Encourage the pupils to observe how the suffix 'ed' is added to each of the base words: for example, do they notice that the final consonant of the word 'hop' is doubled? Help them to understand that the final 'e' of 'hope' is removed before the 'ed' is added, rather than thinking that a letter 'd' is added to the full word. Ask pairs or small groups of children to create two spoken sentences for the different pairs of words.

Sheet B, Look and write: Encourage the children to look closely at the words and to practise writing them.

Sheet B, Listen and write: Dictate each sentence below to the children, emphasising the target words. Encourage the children to copy each sentence in full on the line underneath it. Note that the word 'swimming' is included as revision of adding the suffix 'ing' to words that end with a single consonant. Swimming also appears in Set 34. You could extend the activity by asking the children to make up their own sentence using one or more of the target words.

I laughed as I hopped my way to school.   The swimming pool was shaped like a guitar.
When I reached the top of the mountain I was coated in sweat.   I searched for a notebook with a striped cover.

Name

Date

Look and write

hopped

hoped

laughed

shaped

searched

reached

greeted

coated

waited

striped

Listen and write

I _____ as I _____ my way to school.

_____

The _____ pool was _____ like a guitar.

_____

When I _____ the top of the mountain I was _____ in sweat.

_____

I _____ for a notebook with a _____ cover.

_____

Look, listen and learn

kettle	bottle
middle	giggle
wriggle	little
puddle	table
double	noble

Teacher's notes

Sheet A, Look, listen and learn: Use the words on this page as a focus for discussing phonic patterns and word structures. What do all the words have in common? How do the first seven differ from the final three? Can the children think of other words that feature double 't', double 'd' or double 'g'? Note that where we hear the letter sound (eg the sound /oe/ in noble compared to the /o/ in bottle) and where there are two vowels in the middle (eg the ou in double) we don't have a double consonant before the 'le'. Ask pairs or small groups of children to create two spoken sentences for the different pairs of words.

Sheet B, Look and write: Encourage the children to look closely at the words and to practise writing them.

Sheet B, Listen and write: Dictate each sentence below to the children, emphasising the target words. Encourage the children to copy each sentence in full on the line underneath it. You could extend the activity by asking the children to make up their own sentence using one or more of the target words.

The kettle holds more water than the bottle.   The baby began to wriggle and giggle when she was tickled.
A little puddle appeared below the leak in the roof.   The table is double the height of the bench.

Look and write

kettle

bottle

middle

giggle

wriggle

little

puddle

table

double

noble

Listen and write

The _____ holds more water than the _____.

The baby began to _____ and _____ when she was tickled.

A _____ _____ appeared below the leak in the roof.

The _____ is _____ the height of the bench.

Look, listen and learn

bigger	biggest
larger	largest
narrower	narrowest
wider	widest
thinner	thinnest

Teacher's notes

Sheet A, Look, listen and learn: Use the words on this page as a focus for discussing phonic patterns and word structures. Encourage the pupils to realise that the suffixes 'er' and 'est' are being used to show comparatives. Ask pairs or small groups of children to create two spoken sentences for the different pairs of words.

Sheet B, Look and write: Encourage the children to look closely at the words and to practise writing them.

Sheet B, Listen and write: Dictate each sentence below to the children, emphasising the target words. Can the children apply the rules they have observed to the word 'fattest'? Can they use previously learnt skills to help them to spell grabbed? Encourage the children to copy each sentence in full on the line underneath it. You could extend the activity by asking the children to make up their own sentence using one or more of the target words.

The sponge cake is bigger than the carrot cake but the chocolate cake is the biggest.
The road gets narrower where it crosses the bridge but it soon gets wider again.
The blue pen makes the thinnest line and the red pen makes the fattest.
The greedy boy grabbed the largest sandwich.

Look and write

bigger	biggest
larger	largest
narrower	narrowest
wider	widest
thinner	thinnest

Listen and write

The sponge cake is _____ than the carrot cake but the chocolate cake is the _____.

The road gets _____ where it crosses the bridge but it soon gets _____ again.

The blue pen makes the _____ line and the red pen makes the _____.

The greedy boy _____ the _____ sandwich.

Look, listen and learn

flop	floppy
floppier	floppiest
happier	happiest
funnier	funniest
sun	run

Teacher's notes

Sheet A, Look, listen and learn: Use the words on this page as a focus for discussing phonic patterns and word structures. Encourage the pupils to realise that the suffixes 'er' and 'est' are being used to show comparatives. Are they able to apply previously learnt skills to add these suffixes to words such as 'happy', where the 'y' needs to be replaced with an 'i', and 'fun', where the final consonant needs to be doubled? Ask pairs or small groups of children to create two spoken sentences for the different pairs of words.

Sheet B, Look and write: Encourage the children to look closely at the words and to practise writing them.

Sheet B, Listen and write: Dictate each sentence below to the children, emphasising the target words. Encourage the children to copy each sentence in full on the line underneath it. You could extend the activity by asking the children to make up their own sentence using one or more of the target words.

Mum had a floppy sun hat but my sister's hat was floppier.   The funniest rabbit had the floppiest ears I have ever seen.
I am always happier when the weather is sunny.   The runny honey was runnier than the jam.

Look and write

flop	floppy
floppier	floppiest
happier	happiest
funnier	funniest
sun	run

Listen and write

Mum had a _____ sun hat but my sister's hat was _____.

The _____ rabbit had the _____ ears I have ever seen.

I am always _____ when the weather is _____.

The _____ honey was _____ than the jam.

Look, listen and learn

happily	funnily
warmly	coldly
repeat	repeated
repeatedly	real
really	usual

Teacher's notes

Sheet A, Look, listen and learn: Use the words on this page as a focus for discussing phonic patterns and word structures. Do the children notice how the suffix 'ly' is being added to base words? Are they able to apply previously learnt skills to add 'ly' to words such as 'happy', where the 'y' needs to be replaced with an 'i'? You may wish to point out how the suffix 'ly' is added to words such as real so that the word 'really' has double letter 'l'. Ask pairs or small groups of children to create two spoken sentences for the different pairs of words.

Sheet B, Look and write: Encourage the children to look closely at the words and to practise writing them.

Sheet B, Listen and write: Dictate each sentence below to the children, emphasising the target words. Encourage the children to copy each sentence in full on the line underneath it. Can the children apply their knowledge of how to add 'ly' to base words when they have to spell words such as 'usually'? You could extend the activity by asking the children to make up their own sentence using one or more of the target words.

The audience clapped warmly when the singer sang happily. The teacher looked coldly at the girl who called out repeatedly. I usually read books about real events. I really like speaking funnily.

Look and write

happily

funnily

warmly

coldly

repeat

repeated

repeatedly

real

really

usual

Listen and write

The audience clapped _____ when the singer sang _____ .

The teacher looked _____ at the girl who called out _____ .

I _____ read books about _____ events.

I _____ like speaking _____ .

Look, listen and learn

wonderful	beauty
beautiful	careful
hopeful	useful
wonderfully	beautifully
carefully	usefully

Teacher's notes

Sheet A, Look, listen and learn: Use the words on this page as a focus for discussing phonic patterns and word structures. Note that the suffixes can be added in steps to some of the base words. For example, the suffix 'ful' is added to 'beauty' by removing the final 'y' and replacing it with an 'i', then the suffix 'ly' can be added to 'beautiful'. Ask pairs or small groups of children to create two spoken sentences for the different pairs of words.

Sheet B, Look and write: Encourage the children to look closely at the words and to practise writing them.

Sheet B, Listen and write: Dictate each sentence below to the children, emphasising the target words. You may like to discuss the compound word 'screwdriver'. Encourage the children to copy each sentence in full on the line underneath it. Can the children apply their knowledge of how to add 'ly' to words such as 'careful' when asked to spell 'hopefully'? You could extend the activity by asking the children to make up their own sentence using one or more of the target words.

The wonderful building looked beautiful in the sunlight.   A screwdriver is a very useful tool.
The artist worked both beautifully and carefully.   The dog looked hopefully at his bowl.

Look and write

wonderful	beauty
beautiful	careful
hopeful	useful
wonderfully	beautifully
carefully	usefully

Listen and write

The _____ building looked _____ in the sunlight.

A screwdriver is a very _____ tool.

The artist worked both _____ and _____.

The dog looked _____ at his bowl.

Look, listen and learn

careless	hopeless
meaningless	helpless
useless	carelessly
hopelessly	uselessly
painless	harmless

Teacher's notes

Sheet A, Look, listen and learn: Use the words on this page as a focus for discussing phonic patterns and word structures. Note that the suffixes can be added in steps to some of the base words. For example, the suffix 'less' is added to 'hope' then the suffix 'ly' can be added to 'hopeless'. Ask pairs or small groups of children to create two spoken sentences for the different pairs of words.

Sheet B, Look and write: Encourage the children to look closely at the words and to practise writing them.

Sheet B, Listen and write: Dictate each sentence below to the children, emphasising the target words. Encourage the children to copy each sentence in full on the line underneath it. Can the children remember how to spell 'usually'? You could extend the activity by asking the children to make up their own sentence using one or more of the target words.

"You shouldn't be so careless," said the teacher.
The words on the paper were meaningless to Tim as they were written in French.
Visits to the dentist are usually quite painless.
She threw the paper carelessly towards the bin.

Look and write

careless	hopeless
meaningless	helpless
useless	carelessly
hopelessly	uselessly
painless	harmless

Listen and write

"You shouldn't be so _____," said the teacher.

The words on the paper were _____ to Tim as they were written in French.

Visits to the dentist are _____ quite _____.

She threw the paper _____ towards the bin.

Look, listen and learn

it's	we'll
we've	we're
isn't	can't
haven't	doesn't
won't	they're

Teacher's notes

Sheet A, Look, listen and learn: Use the words on this page as a focus for discussing phonic patterns and word structures. All of these words feature the use of an apostrophe to replace missing letters when two words are joined together. Which words have only one missing letter? Which words have two missing letters? Which word is completely changed? Ask pairs or small groups of children to create two spoken sentences for the different pairs of words.

Sheet B, Look and write: Encourage the children to look closely at the words and to practise writing them.

Sheet B, Listen and write: Dictate each sentence below to the children, emphasising the target words. Encourage the children to copy each sentence in full on the line underneath it. You could extend the activity by asking the children to make up their own sentence using one or more of the target words.

We've worked for hours and we haven't had a break.
The Reception children have got boots on because they're going for a walk.
The weather isn't very nice but the forecast says it's going to be better later.
My friend doesn't like singing but we'll have to sing in the concert.

Name   Date

Look and write

it's	we'll
we've	we're
isn't	can't
haven't	doesn't
won't	they're

Listen and write

_____ worked for hours and we _____ had a break.

The Reception children have got boots on because _____ going for a walk.

The weather _____ very nice but the forecast says _____ going to be better later.

My friend _____ like singing but _____ have to sing in the concert.

Look, listen and learn

cat's	cats'
boy's	boys'
girl's	girls'
child's	children's
woman's	women's

Teacher's notes

Sheet A, Look, listen and learn: Use the words on this page as a focus for discussing phonic patterns and word structures. All of these words feature the use of an apostrophe to show ownership. Encourage the children to notice that the apostrophe appears after the 'owner' or 'owners'. For example, the apostrophe in cat's shows that there is one cat whereas the apsotrophe in cats' shows there is more than one cat. Ask pairs or small groups of children to create two spoken sentences for the different pairs of words.

Sheet B, Look and write: Encourage the children to look closely at the words and to practise writing them.

Sheet B, Listen and write: Dictate each sentence below to the children, emphasising the target words. Encourage the children to copy each sentence in full on the line underneath it. You could extend the activity by asking the children to make up their own sentence using one or more of the target words.

My cat's coat is white but my friends two cats' coats are black.
One boy's shoes were clean but all the other boys' shoes were muddy.
The girl's bag fell off the shelf and knocked over the other girls' drinks.
The women's magazines were on a higher shelf than the children's magazines.

Look and write

cat's	cats'
boy's	boys'
girl's	girls'
child's	children's
woman's	women's

Listen and write

My _____ coat is white but my friends two _____ coats are black.

_____

One _____ shoes were clean but all the other _____ shoes were muddy.

_____

The _____ bag fell off the shelf and knocked over the other _____ drinks.

_____

The _____ magazines were on a higher shelf than the _____ magazines.

_____

Look, listen and learn

right	fright
bright	brighter
brighten	frighten
frightening	high
height	flight

Teacher's notes

Sheet A, Look, listen and learn: Use the words on this page as a focus for discussing phonic patterns and word structures. All of these words contain the grapheme 'igh' representing the phoneme /ie/. Note that some of the words feature suffixes. Ask pairs or small groups of children to create two spoken sentences for the different pairs of words.

Sheet B, Look and write: Encourage the children to look closely at the words and to practise writing them.

Sheet B, Listen and write: Dictate each sentence below to the children, emphasising the target words. Encourage the children to copy each sentence in full on the line underneath it. Point out the spelling of the name 'Wright' and the use of the apostrophe after the word brothers' (showing ownership by both brothers). You could extend the activity by asking the children to make up their own sentence using one or more of the target words.

The sudden bright light was quite frightening.   The Wright brothers' first flight reached a height of only three metres.
My mum likes to brighten up the day by singing loudly!   The sun is coming out and brightening up the morning.

Look and write

right

fright

bright

brighter

brighten

frighten

frightening

high

height

flight

Listen and write

The sudden _____ _____ was quite _____.

_____

The Wright brothers' first _____ reached a _____ of only three metres.

_____

My mum likes to _____ up the day by singing loudly!

_____

The sun is coming out and _____ up the morning.

_____

Look, listen and learn

cough	tough
enough	ought
bought	though
through	thought
bough	brought

Teacher's notes

Sheet A, Look, listen and learn: Use the words on this page as a focus for discussing phonic patterns and word structures. All of these words contain the grapheme 'ough' – can the children identify all the phonemes that this grapheme represents? For example, in the word 'cough' the 'ough' represents the phonemes /o/ /f/, in the word 'tough' it represents the phonemes /u/ /f/, in the word 'ought' it represents the phoneme /or/, etc. Ask pairs or small groups of children to create two spoken sentences for the different pairs of words.

Sheet B, Look and write: Encourage the children to look closely at the words and to practise writing them.

Sheet B, Listen and write: Dictate each sentence below to the children, emphasising the target words. Encourage the children to copy each sentence in full on the line underneath it. Can the children remember the use of the apostrophe in the revised word haven't? You could extend the activity by asking the children to make up their own sentence using one or more of the target words.

I thought I heard a loud cough.   The teacher bought some new books for the school library.
It was very tough to climb to the highest bough of the tree.   I thought I brought my PE kit today but I haven't.

     Andrew Brodie: Improving Spelling for Ages 8–9 © A&C Black, Bloomsbury Publishing 2011

Look and write

cough	tough
enough	ought
bought	though
through	thought
bough	brought

Listen and write

I _____ I heard a loud _____ .

_____

The teacher _____ some new books for the school library.

_____

It was very _____ to climb to the highest _____ of the tree.

_____

I _____ I _____ my PE kit today but I _____ .

_____

Look, listen and learn

laugh	laughing
laughed	daughter
teach	teacher
taught	catch
catching	caught

Teacher's notes

Sheet A, Look, listen and learn: Use the words on this page as a focus for discussing phonic patterns and word structures. All of these words contain the grapheme 'augh' – can the children identify both the phonemes that this grapheme represents? For example, in the word 'laugh' the 'augh' represents the phonemes /a/ /f/ (or /ar/ /f/ in some southern regions), in the word 'taught' it represents the phoneme /or/. Ask pairs or small groups of children to create two spoken sentences for the different pairs of words.

Sheet B, Look and write: Encourage the children to look closely at the words and to practise writing them.

Sheet B, Listen and write: Dictate each sentence below to the children, emphasising the target words. Encourage the children to copy each sentence in full on the line underneath it. You could extend the activity by asking the children to make up their own sentence using one or more of the target words.

My daughter laughed when I tried to catch the ball.   I'm not very good at catching but I caught a cold quite easily!
Some children were laughing when the teachers were dancing in the show.   The teacher taught us the four times table.

Name   Date

Look and write

laugh

laughing

laughed

daughter

teach

teacher

taught

catch

catching

caught

Listen and write

My _____ _____ when I tried to _____ the ball.

I'm not very good at _____ but I _____ a cold quite easily!

Some children were _____ when the _____ were dancing in the show.

The _____ _____ us the four times table.

Look, listen and learn

wallet	warm
wall	wander
want	watch
waste	water
wave	wax

Teacher's notes

Sheet A, Look, listen and learn: Use the words on this page as a focus for discussing phonic patterns and word structures. All of these words start with the letters 'wa' but ask the children what sounds are being made by the letter 'a' in each word – note that in the word 'warm' the 'a' is combined with the 'r' to represent the phoneme /or/. Ask pairs or small groups of children to create two spoken sentences for the different pairs of words.

Sheet B, Look and write: Encourage the children to look closely at the words and to practise writing them.

Sheet B, Listen and write: Dictate each sentence below to the children, emphasising the target words. Encourage the children to copy each sentence in full on the line underneath it. You could extend the activity by asking the children to make up their own sentence using one or more of the target words.

The wall by the radiator is always quite warm.   I put my watch and my wallet in the locker.
It's important not to waste water.   All the people were waving when the prince went past.

Look and write

wallet	warm
wall	wander
want	watch
waste	water
wave	wax

Listen and write

The _____ by the radiator is always quite _____.

_____

I put my _____ and my _____ in the locker.

_____

It's important not to _____ _____.

_____

All the people were _____ when the prince went past.

_____

Look, listen and learn

wobble

woke

woman

women

wonder

won't

wool

word

worn

worry

Teacher's notes

Sheet A, Look, listen and learn: Use the words on this page as a focus for discussing phonic patterns and word structures. All of these words start with the letters 'wo' but ask the children what sounds are being made by the letter 'o' in each word – note that in the word 'worn' the 'o' is combined with the 'r' to represent the phoneme /or/ but in word the same combination represents /ur/. Ask pairs or small groups of children to create two spoken sentences for the different pairs of words.

Sheet B, Look and write: Encourage the children to look closely at the words and to practise writing them.

Sheet B, Listen and write: Dictate each sentence below to the children, emphasising the target words. The use of the apostrophe can be revised in the word I've. Encourage the children to copy each sentence in full on the line underneath it. You could extend the activity by asking the children to make up their own sentence using one or more of the target words.

Try not to wobble when you ride your bike.   When the woman woke she began to worry about all the work she had to do.
The wool on my jumper has worn into a hole.   I wonder where I've put my book.

Look and write

wobble

woke

woman

women

wonder

won't

wool

word

worn

worry

Listen and write

Try not to _____ when you ride your bike.

_____

When the _____ _____ she began to _____

about all the _____ she had to do.

_____

_____

The _____ on my jumper has _____ into a hole.

_____

I _____ where I've put my book.

_____

Look, listen and learn

boss	floss
passage	possible
impossible	possibility
impossibility	possibilities
guess	guessing

Teacher's notes

Sheet A, Look, listen and learn: Use the words on this page as a focus for discussing phonic patterns and word structures. All of these words include the double letter 's'. The pupils will need help to observe the spellings of the difficult words 'guess' and 'guessing' and the words derived from the base word possible. Ask pairs or small groups of children to create two spoken sentences for the different pairs of words.

Sheet B, Look and write: Encourage the children to look closely at the words and to practise writing them.

Sheet B, Listen and write: Dictate each sentence below to the children, emphasising the target words and the revision words. Encourage the children to copy each sentence in full on the line underneath it. You could extend the activity by asking the children to make up their own sentence using one or more of the target words.

The boss said the job was impossible.   Some people floss their teeth every day.
Can you guess how many children are in this school?   Flying to the sun is an impossibility.

Name   Date

Look and write

boss

floss

passage

possible

impossible

possibility

impossibility

possibilities

guess

guessing

Listen and write

The _____ said the job was _____.

Some people _____ their teeth every day.

Can you _____ how many _____ are in this school?

_____ to the sun is an _____.

Look, listen and learn

page	cage
stage	teenager
teenaged	passage
carriage	marriage
bridge	fridge

Sheet A, Look, listen and learn: Use the words on this page as a focus for discussing phonic patterns and word structures. All of these words feature the phoneme /j/, represented by the grapheme 'ge' or the grapheme 'dge'. The pupils will need help to observe the spellings of the difficult words 'carriage' and 'marriage'. Ask pairs or small groups of children to create two spoken sentences for the different pairs of words.

Sheet B, Look and write: Encourage the children to look closely at the words and to practise writing them.

Sheet B, Listen and write: Dictate each sentence below to the children, emphasising the target words and the revision words. Encourage the children to copy each sentence in full on the line underneath it. You could extend the activity by asking the children to make up their own sentence using one or more of the target words.

> After the marriage the prince and princess went to the palace in a carriage.
> My sister is a teenager and she likes to appear on the stage.
> There's a picture of a bridge on the front page of the geography book.
> The teacher read a short passage from the book.

Look and write

page

cage

stage

teenager

teenaged

passage

carriage

marriage

bridge

fridge

Listen and write

After the _____ the prince and princess went to the palace in a

_____ .

_____

My sister is a _____ and she likes to appear on the _____ .

_____

There's a picture of a _____ on the front _____ of the

geography book.

_____

The teacher read a short _____ from the book.

_____

Look, listen and learn

about	found
ground	amount
couch	crouch
ouch	loud
cloud	proud

Look and write

about

found

ground

amount

couch

crouch

ouch

loud

cloud

proud

Listen and write

I _____ a _____ on the _____ .

I had to _____ out a large _____ of money.

"_____!" said the boy _____ when he fell off the

_____ .

A big white _____ made a shadow on the _____ .

Look, listen and learn

blot	plot
knot	squat
swat	what
yacht	dotted
spot	spotted

Teacher's notes

Sheet A, Look, listen and learn: Use the words on this page as a focus for discussing phonic patterns and word structures. All of these words feature the combination of the phonemes /o/ and /t/. Ask the children to sort the words into groups according to how the phoneme combination is spelt. Which is the strangest spelling do they think? Ask pairs or small groups of children to create two spoken sentences for the different pairs of words.

Sheet B, Look and write: Encourage the children to look closely at the words and to practise writing them.

Sheet B, Listen and write: Dictate each sentence below to the children, emphasising the target words and the revision word girl's, which features an apostrophe for ownership. Encourage the children to copy each sentence in full on the line underneath it. You could extend the activity by asking the children to make up their own sentence using one or more of the target words.

The girl's book was dotted with ink blots.   I spotted a large yacht out at sea.
In PE we had to squat then jump up.   He tried to swat the fly with a knotted handkerchief.

Look and write

blot	plot
knot	squat
swat	what
yacht	dotted
spot	spotted

Listen and write

The _____ book was _____ with ink _____.

_____

I _____ a large _____ out at sea.

_____

In PE we had to _____ then jump up.

_____

He tried to _____ the fly with a _____ handkerchief.

_____

Look, listen and learn

haul	autumn
taught	caught
aunt	auntie
aunty	cause
because	sausage

Teacher's notes

Sheet A, Look, listen and learn: Use the words on this page as a focus for discussing phonic patterns and word structures. Many of these words feature the phoneme /or/, represented by the grapheme 'au' but the same grapheme represents a different phoneme in the words 'aunt' and 'auntie' (alternative spelling 'aunty'): in some regions the phoneme is /a/ and in others it is /ar/. Ask pairs or small groups of children to create two spoken sentences for the different pairs of words.

Sheet B, Look and write: Encourage the children to look closely at the words and to practise writing them.

Sheet B, Listen and write: Dictate each sentence below to the children, emphasising the target words and the revision words. Note that some of the words are derivatives of the base words. Encourage the children to copy each sentence in full on the line underneath it. You could extend the activity by asking the children to make up their own sentence using one or more of the target words.

We hauled the rope to pull the bow of the yacht.   In the autumn my aunt taught me how to dive.
The boy ate three sausages and a huge pile of chips because he was so hungry.   The rain caused the fire to go out.

Look and write

haul	autumn
taught	caught
aunt	auntie
aunty	cause
because	sausage

Listen and write

We _____ the rope to pull the bow of the _____ .

_____

In the _____ my _____ _____ me how to dive.

_____

The boy ate three _____ and a huge pile of chips _____ he was so hungry.

_____

_____

The rain _____ the fire to go out.

_____

Look, listen and learn

double	trouble
four	fourteen
forty	pour
young	younger
youngest	journey

Teacher's notes

Sheet A, Look, listen and learn: Use the words on this page as a focus for discussing phonic patterns and word structures. Most of these words feature the grapheme 'ou' but the word 'forty' is also included to show how its spelling contrasts with the spelling of 'four' and 'fourteen'. Ask pairs or small groups of children to create two spoken sentences for the different pairs of words.

Sheet B, Look and write: Encourage the children to look closely at the words and to practise writing them.

Sheet B, Listen and write: Dictate each sentence below to the children, emphasising the target words and the revision words. Encourage the children to copy each sentence in full on the line underneath it. You could extend the activity by asking the children to make up their own sentence using one or more of the target words.

Mum said the twins are double trouble!
My brother is four, my sister is fourteen and my mum is forty.
My brother is the youngest member of my family and I am younger than my sister.
The journey took double the time that I expected.

 Andrew Brodie: Improving Spelling for Ages 8–9 © A&C Black, Bloomsbury Publishing 2011

Look and write

double

trouble

four

fourteen

forty

pour

young

younger

youngest

journey

Listen and write

Mum said the twins are _____ _____!

_____

My brother is _____, my sister is _____ and my mum
is _____.

_____

My brother is the _____ member of my family and I am
_____ than my sister.

_____

The _____ took _____ the time that I expected.

_____

Look, listen and learn

motorway	birthday
underwater	waterproof
overcrowded	overhead
overload	overnight
undercover	underground

Teacher's notes

Sheet A, Look, listen and learn: Use the words on this page as a focus for discussing phonic patterns and word structures. Do the children notice that all the words are compound words, ie each word is made from a combination of two others? Ask pairs or small groups of children to create two spoken sentences for the different pairs of words.

Sheet B, Look and write: Encourage the children to look closely at the words and to practise writing them.

Sheet B, Listen and write: Dictate each sentence below to the children, emphasising the target words and the revision words. Encourage the children to copy each sentence in full on the line underneath it. You could extend the activity by asking the children to make up their own sentence using one or more of the target words.

The swimming pool was overcrowded so I spent most of my time swimming underwater.
There was a lot of rain overnight so I'm glad the tent was waterproof.
The spy was working undercover.
Unfortunately we spent hours on the motorway on my birthday.

Look and write

motorway	birthday
underwater	waterproof
overcrowded	overhead
overload	overnight
undercover	underground

Listen and write

The swimming pool was _____ so I spent most of my time

swimming _____ .

_____

_____

There was a lot of rain _____ so I'm glad the tent was

_____ .

_____

The spy was working _____ .

_____

Unfortunately we spent hours on the _____ on my

_____ .

_____

Look, listen and learn

terrible	horrible
terribly	horribly
responsible	responsibly
reversible	visible
invisible	edible

Teacher's notes

Sheet A, Look, listen and learn: Use the words on this page as a focus for discussing phonic patterns and word structures. Do the children notice that most of the words end with 'ible' and that some have the suffix 'ly'? Encourage them to understand that the ending 'le' has been replaced by the suffix 'ly', rather than considering that the final 'e' has been replaced by a 'y'. Ask pairs or small groups of children to create two spoken sentences for the different pairs of words.

Sheet B, Look and write: Encourage the children to look closely at the words and to practise writing them.

Sheet B, Listen and write: Dictate each sentence below to the children, emphasising the target words and the revision words. Encourage the children to copy each sentence in full on the line underneath it. You could extend the activity by asking the children to make up their own sentence using one or more of the target words.

I try hard with my writing but sometimes it looks terrible.   "Are you responsible for this horrible mess?" asked the teacher.
My coat is reversible so I can decide which colour I want to be visible.   The spy wrote the message using invisible ink.

Look and write

terrible	horrible
terribly	horribly
responsible	responsibly
reversible	visible
invisible	edible

Listen and write

I try hard with my writing but sometimes it looks _____.

"Are you _____ for this _____ mess?" asked the teacher.

My coat is _____ so I can decide which colour I want to be

_____.

The spy wrote the message using _____ ink.

Look, listen and learn

laughable	break
broke	broken
breakable	value
valuable	enjoy
enjoyable	enjoyment

Teacher's notes

Sheet A, Look, listen and learn: Use the words on this page as a focus for discussing phonic patterns and word structures. Encourage the pupils to observe the relationships between the base words and their derivatives – the words derived from 'break' are particularly interesting. Ask pairs or small groups of children to create two spoken sentences for the different pairs of words.

Sheet B, Look and write: Encourage the children to look closely at the words and to practise writing them.

Sheet B, Listen and write: Dictate each sentence below to the children, emphasising the target words and the revision words. Encourage the children to copy each sentence in full on the line underneath it. You could extend the activity by asking the children to make up their own sentence using one or more of the target words.

My attempt at winning the race was laughable!   I didn't think the flask was breakable but I broke it!
Try not to break the vase because it's quite valuable.   The children gain lots of enjoyment from playing in the sand.

Andrew Brodie: Improving Spelling for Ages 8–9 © A&C Black, Bloomsbury Publishing 2011

Look and write

laughable

break

broke

broken

breakable

value

valuable

enjoy

enjoyable

enjoyment

Listen and write

My attempt at _____ the race was _____!

I didn't think the flask was _____ but I _____ it!

Try not to _____ the vase because it's quite _____.

The _____ gain lots of _____ from _____ in the sand.

Look, listen and learn

station	nation
national	pollute
polluted	pollution
information	education
relation	educational

Teacher's notes

Sheet A, Look, listen and learn: Use the words on this page as a focus for discussing phonic patterns and word structures. Are the children familiar with the letter string 'tion' representing the phonemes /sh/ /u/ /n/? Encourage the pupils to observe the relationships between the base words and their derivatives. Ask pairs or small groups of children to create two spoken sentences for the different pairs of words.

Sheet B, Look and write: Encourage the children to look closely at the words and to practise writing them.

Sheet B, Listen and write: Dictate each sentence below to the children, emphasising the target words and the revision words. Encourage the children to copy each sentence in full on the line underneath it. You could extend the activity by asking the children to make up their own sentence using one or more of the target words.

The local station is part of the national network of railways.   The river was polluted with chemicals.
We learn a lot of information through our education.   Television is sometimes very educational.

Look and write

station

nation

national

pollute

polluted

pollution

information

education

relation

educational

Listen and write

The local _____ is part of the _____ network of railways.

The river was _____ with chemicals.

We learn a lot of _____ through our _____.

Television is sometimes very _____.

Look, listen and learn

addition	subtract
subtraction	multiply
multiplication	divide
division	calculate
calculation	calculating

Teacher's notes

Sheet A, Look, listen and learn: Use the words on this page as a focus for discussing phonic patterns and word structures. The pupils will notice that all the words are related to maths but some of them also have the letter string 'tion' in common, representing the phonemes /sh/ /u/ /n/. Do they notice that 'division' ends differently? Can they think of other words that end with 'sion'? Ask pairs or small groups of children to create two spoken sentences for the different pairs of words.

Sheet B, Look and write: Encourage the children to look closely at the words and to practise writing them.

Sheet B, Listen and write: Dictate each sentence below to the children, emphasising the target words. Point out that the word 'calculator' is related to the base word 'calculate' – can the children add the suffix 'or' correctly? Encourage the children to copy each sentence in full on the line underneath it. You could extend the activity by asking the children to make up their own sentence using one or more of the target words.

In maths we work on addition and subtraction.   Most people find division harder than multiplication.
It is easier to divide if you know how to multiply.   Some people use a calculator for calculating.

Look and write

addition

subtract

subtraction

multiply

multiplication

divide

division

calculate

calculation

calculating

Listen and write

In maths we work on _____ and _____ .

_____

Most people find _____ harder than _____ .

_____

It is easier to _____ if you know how to _____ .

_____

Some people use a _____ for _____ .

_____

Look, listen and learn

revision	explosion
confuse	confused
confusion	decision
invasion	tension
extension	mansion

Teacher's notes

Sheet A, Look, listen and learn: Use the words on this page as a focus for discussing phonic patterns and word structures. Can the pupils observe the links between base words and their derivatives with the 'sion' suffix? Do they notice that the base words usually end with 'se' or 'de'? Ask pairs or small groups of children to create two spoken sentences for the different pairs of words.

Sheet B, Look and write: Encourage the children to look closely at the words and to practise writing them.

Sheet B, Listen and write: Dictate each sentence below to the children, emphasising the target words. Encourage the children to copy each sentence in full on the line underneath it. You could extend the activity by asking the children to make up their own sentence using one or more of the target words.

There was a loud explosion at the quarry.   My sister does her revision in our extension.
I was confused about maths so I made the decision to ask the teacher.   The Norman invasion of England was in 1066.

Name   Date

Look and write

revision

explosion

confuse

confused

confusion

decision

invasion

tension

extension

mansion

Listen and write

There was a loud _____ at the quarry.

_____

My sister does her _____ in our _____.

_____

I was _____ about maths so I made the _____ to ask
the teacher.

_____

The Norman _____ of England was in 1066.

_____

Look, listen and learn

infect	infection
infectious	delicious
vicious	ambition
ambitious	reflect
reflected	reflection

Teacher's notes

Sheet A, Look, listen and learn: Use the words on this page as a focus for discussing phonic patterns and word structures. Can the pupils observe the links between base words and their derivatives with the suffixes 'ed', 'tion' or 'tious'? Do they notice that the two words 'delicious' and 'vicious' are odd ones out? Ask pairs or small groups of children to create two spoken sentences for the different pairs of words.

Sheet B, Look and write: Encourage the children to look closely at the words and to practise writing them.

Sheet B, Listen and write: Dictate each sentence below to the children, emphasising the target words. Note that the sentences also include two words with the ending 'or'. Encourage the children to copy each sentence in full on the line underneath it. You could extend the activity by asking the children to make up their own sentence using one or more of the target words.

I was sneezing a lot when I had an infectious cold.　The chocolate cake was delicious.
My ambition is to be an actor.　I saw my reflection in the mirror.

Look and write

infect	infection
infectious	delicious
vicious	ambition
ambitious	reflect
reflected	reflection

Listen and write

I was sneezing a lot when I had an _____ cold.

The chocolate cake was _____.

My _____ is to be an _____.

I saw my _____ in the _____.

Look, listen and learn

quick	quicker
quickly	ticket
cricket	cricketer
tickle	trickle
prickle	prickly

Look and write

quick	quicker
quickly	ticket
cricket	cricketer
tickle	trickle
prickle	prickly

Listen and write

The _____ ran _____ but he wasn't _____ enough.

The _____ of water felt very _____ as it went down my neck.

The _____ on the holly bush were very _____.

I think _____ is _____.

Look, listen and learn

swim

swimming

swimmer

swam

trim

trimming

trimmer

trimmed

glimmer

skim

Teacher's notes

Sheet A, Look, listen and learn: Use the words on this page as a focus for discussing phonic patterns and word structures. Do the children recognise the similarities in the words? Ask them to compare the past tense of 'swim' to the past tense versions of 'trim' and 'skim'. Ask pairs or small groups of children to create two spoken sentences for the different pairs of words.

Sheet B, Look and write: Encourage the children to look closely at the words and to practise writing them.

Sheet B, Listen and write: Dictate each sentence below to the children, emphasising the target words and the revision words. Encourage the children to copy each sentence in full on the line underneath it. You could extend the activity by asking the children to make up their own sentence using one or more of the target words.

The swimmer swam strongly across the glimmering water.
I can skim stones across water.
I needed to trim the paper to the right size so I trimmed it with scissors.
The water skier was skimming along the surface of the water, avoiding the swimmers.

Look and write

swim	swimming
swimmer	swam
trim	trimming
trimmer	trimmed
glimmer	skim

Listen and write

The _____ strongly across the _____ water.

I can _____ stones across water.

I needed to _____ the paper to the right size so I _____ it with scissors.

The water skier was _____ along the surface of the water, avoiding the _____ .

Look, listen and learn

miscalculate	mislead
nonsense	non-fiction
non-iron	impossible
exchange	inactive
co-star	anticlockwise

Teacher's notes

Sheet A, Look, listen and learn: Use the words on this page as a focus for discussing phonic patterns and word structures. Do the pupils notice that all of the words feature prefixes and that some of these need hyphens? Can they think of other words that start with the same prefixes? Ask pairs or small groups of children to create two spoken sentences for the different pairs of words.

Sheet B, Look and write: Encourage the children to look closely at the words and to practise writing them.

Sheet B, Listen and write: Dictate each sentence below to the children, emphasising the target words and the revision words. Encourage the children to copy each sentence in full on the line underneath it. You could extend the activity by asking the children to make up their own sentence using one or more of the target words.

I made a mistake in my maths when I miscalculated the addition.   The teacher said that the boy's story was nonsense.
Some people prefer non-fiction to fiction books.   The runners went in an anticlockwise direction around the track.

Look and write

miscalculate	mislead
nonsense	non-fiction
non-iron	impossible
exchange	inactive
co-star	anticlockwise

Listen and write

I made a mistake in my maths when I _____ the

_____ .

_____

The teacher said that the _____ story was _____ .

_____

Some people prefer _____ to _____ books.

_____

The _____ went in an _____ direction around the track.

_____

_____

Andrew Brodie: Improving Spelling for Ages 8–9 © A&C Black, Bloomsbury Publishing 2011

Look, listen and learn

| bicycle | recalculate |

| tricycle | abnormal |

| rearrange | prearrange |

| precast | prejudge |

| preschool | preview |

Look and write

bicycle

recalculate

tricycle

abnormal

rearrange

prearrange

precast

prejudge

preschool

preview

Listen and write

When I was small I had a _____ but now I have a _____ .

It would be _____ to wear shoes in bed!

Can we _____ the meeting that we had _____ for this afternoon?

I'm not going to _____ the film until I've seen a _____ of it.

Look, listen and learn

unusual	unusually
untrue	unhappy
unhappily	unknown
unless	unlikely
unlocked	unlucky

Teacher's notes

Sheet A, Look, listen and learn: Use the words on this page as a focus for discussing phonic patterns and word structures. All of these words feature the prefix 'un' but several also have suffixes that have been seen in previous lists. Ask pairs or small groups of children to create two spoken sentences for the different pairs of words.

Sheet B, Look and write: Encourage the children to look closely at the words and to practise writing them.

Sheet B, Listen and write: Dictate each sentence below to the children, emphasising the target words. Encourage the children to copy each sentence in full on the line underneath it. You could extend the activity by asking the children to make up their own sentence using one or more of the target words.

It is very unusual to have rainy weather in the desert.   I hope you are not unhappy with your spelling test results.
Unhappily you will miss break-time, unless you get on with your work!   It is unlikely that the front door is unlocked.

Look and write

unusual

unusually

untrue

unhappy

unhappily

unknown

unless

unlikely

unlocked

unlucky

Listen and write

It is very _____ to have _____ weather in the desert.

_____

I hope you are not _____ with your spelling test results.

_____

_____ you will miss break-time, _____ you get on with

your work!

_____

_____

It is _____ that the front door is _____ .

_____

Look, listen and learn

disinfect

disobey

disobeyed

disobedient

disqualify

deforest

decode

debug

deflate

defrost

Teacher's notes

Sheet A, Look, listen and learn: Use the words on this page as a focus for discussing phonic patterns and word structures. Do the pupils notice that all of the words feature prefixes? Can they think of other words that start with the same prefixes? Ask pairs or small groups of children to create two spoken sentences for the different pairs of words.

Sheet B, Look and write: Encourage the children to look closely at the words and to practise writing them.

Sheet B, Listen and write: Dictate each sentence below to the children, emphasising the target words and the word properly, which revises the suffix 'ly'. Encourage the children to copy each sentence in full on the line underneath it. You could extend the activity by asking the children to make up their own sentence using one or more of the target words.

We should disinfect the kitchen surfaces every day.   The dog was very disobedient and always disobeyed his owner.
Mum had to debug the computer because it wasn't working properly.   We had to deflate the boat to pack it in the car.

Andrew Brodie: Improving Spelling for Ages 8–9 © A&C Black, Bloomsbury Publishing 2011

Look and write

disinfect

disobey

disobeyed

disobedient

disqualify

deforest

decode

debug

deflate

defrost

Listen and write

We should _____ the kitchen surfaces every day.

The dog was very _____ and always _____ his owner.

Mum had to _____ the computer because it wasn't working
_____ .

We had to _____ the boat to pack it in the car.

Look, listen and learn

interactive	interlocking
interior	exterior
international	internet
submarine	subtitle
subtract	suburbs

Teacher's notes

Sheet A, Look, listen and learn: Use the words on this page as a focus for discussing phonic patterns and word structures. Do the pupils notice that all of the words feature prefixes? Can they think of other words that start with the same prefixes? Note that some words feature prefixes that cannot be removed – for example, removing the prefix 'sub' from subtract does not leave a complete word but it is a Latin prefix. Ask pairs or small groups of children to create two spoken sentences for the different pairs of words.

Sheet B, Look and write: Encourage the children to look closely at the words and to practise writing them.

Sheet B, Listen and write: Dictate each sentence below to the children, emphasising the target words. Ensure that the children understand the meaning of words such as suburbs. Encourage the children to copy each sentence in full on the line underneath it. You could extend the activity by asking the children to make up their own sentence using one or more of the target words.

The exterior of the house was built with interlocking bricks.   The interior of the submarine is very cramped.
Houses in the suburbs often have large gardens.   We watched the international match on the internet.

Look and write

interactive

interlocking

interior

exterior

international

internet

submarine

subtitle

subtract

suburbs

Listen and write

The _____ of the house was built with _____ bricks.

The _____ of the _____ is very cramped.

Houses in the _____ often have large gardens.

We watched the _____ match on the _____ .

Look, listen and learn

happiness	carelessness
silliness	craziness
madness	friendship
hardship	spaceship
membership	premiership

Teacher's notes

Sheet A, Look, listen and learn: Use the words on this page as a focus for discussing phonic patterns and word structures. Do the pupils notice that all of the words feature suffixes? Can they think of other words that end with the same suffixes? Ask pairs or small groups of children to create two spoken sentences for the different pairs of words.

Sheet B, Look and write: Encourage the children to look closely at the words and to practise writing them.

Sheet B, Listen and write: Dictate each sentence below to the children, emphasising the target words and the revision words. Encourage the children to copy each sentence in full on the line underneath it. You could extend the activity by asking the children to make up their own sentence using one or more of the target words.

Good friendship brings great happiness.   The football club gained membership of the premiership.
"There's been too much silliness this morning," said the teacher.   Mistakes are often caused by carelessness.

    Andrew Brodie: Improving Spelling for Ages 8–9 © A&C Black, Bloomsbury Publishing 2011

Look and write

happiness

carelessness

silliness

craziness

madness

friendship

hardship

spaceship

membership

premiership

Listen and write

Good _____ brings great _____ .

_____

The football club gained _____ of the _____ .

_____

" _____ been too much _____ this morning," said the teacher.

_____

Mistakes are often caused by _____ .

_____

Look, listen and learn

childhood	neighbourhood
expense	expensive
compete	competitive
attract	attractive
active	activity

Teacher's notes

Sheet A, Look, listen and learn: Use the words on this page as a focus for discussing phonic patterns and word structures. Do the pupils notice that some of the words feature suffixes and that some of the base words are shown? Can they add extra suffixes, such as 'ly' to 'expensive'? Ask pairs or small groups of children to create two spoken sentences for the different pairs of words.

Sheet B, Look and write: Encourage the children to look closely at the words and to practise writing them.

Sheet B, Listen and write: Dictate each sentence below to the children, emphasising the target words and the compound word secondhand. Encourage the children to copy each sentence in full on the line underneath it. You could extend the activity by asking the children to make up their own sentence using one or more of the target words.

I spent my childhood in a friendly neighbourhood.   A new bike was too expensive so I had a secondhand one.
My sister is very competitive and is always competing with me.   Try to attract attention to the best activity.

Look and write

childhood

neighbourhood

expense

expensive

compete

competitive

attract

attractive

active

activity

Listen and write

I spent my _____ in a friendly _____ .

_____

A new bike was too _____ so I had a _____ one.

_____

_____

My sister is very _____ and is always _____ with me.

_____

Try to _____ attention to the best _____ .

_____

Look, listen and learn

metre	centimetre
millimetre	kilometre
litre	millilitre
centilitre	gram
milligram	kilogram

Teacher's notes

Sheet A, Look, listen and learn: Use the words on this page as a focus for discussing phonic patterns and word structures. All of these words are related to measurement. Encourage the pupils to observe the addition of the prefixes 'centi', 'milli' and 'kilo' to the base words. Are they aware that 'centi' represents one hundredth of the base unit, 'milli' represents one thousandth of the base unit and 'kilo' represents one thousand of the base unit? Ask pairs or small groups of children to create two spoken sentences for the different pairs of words.

Sheet B, Look and write: Encourage the children to look closely at the words and to practise writing them.

Sheet B, Listen and write: Dictate each sentence below to the children, emphasising the target words. Encourage the children to copy each sentence in full on the line underneath it. You could extend the activity by asking the children to make up their own sentence using one or more of the target words.

My brother is a few centimetres less than a metre tall.   One kilometre is a thousand metres.
There are a thousand milligrams in one gram.   There are five hundred millilitres in half a litre.

Andrew Brodie: Improving Spelling for Ages 8–9 © A&C Black, Bloomsbury Publishing 2011

Name   Date

Look and write

| metre | centimetre |

| millimetre | kilometre |

| litre | millilitre |

| centilitre | gram |

| milligram | kilogram |

Listen and write

My brother is a few _____ less than a _____ tall.

_____

One _____ is a thousand _____.

_____

There are a thousand _____ in one _____.

_____

There are five hundred _____ in half a _____.

_____

Assessment 1

On my **birthday** my mum and I went for a walk **alongside** the **river**. We went past the **hospital** and the **college** then **reached** the **cricket** ground. We **stopped** for a while to **watch** the **match**. When we realised that we **didn't** know how to play the game, we **laughed** and **walked** on.

The path became **narrower** as it passed through lots of **bushes**. It became **wider** again as we left the town **behind**. Now we were in the countryside we **could** see for miles. There were some **people** riding **ponies** but they **seemed** a long way **away**. They **couldn't** have been too far **though** because a couple of minutes later I was quite **frightened** when they galloped past us.

What could happen next in this story?

Assessment 2

My sister is a **teenager** and she's **horrible** to me! She's **fourteen** years old and I'm only nine so **because** I'm **younger** she thinks she can do **terrible** things and get away with them. One day I went into my **bedroom** and **found** that she had tied a **knot** in every one of my socks! I was so **cross** that I took all her socks and hid them where she **couldn't possibly** find them – I put them **underneath** the sofa.

Later that day we were both **sitting** on the sofa **watching** television. I **remembered** the socks and began **laughing**.

"What are you **giggling** about?" she **asked**.

"Nothing," I **replied**.

What could happen next in this story?

Assessment 3

When I was **younger** I had a red **tricycle** but now I have a blue **bicycle**. I like to think that my bike is quite **unusual** because when I'm on it I can fly. It's **true**!

Yesterday I was **riding** to see my **friend**. I was **quite** late so I began pedalling really **quickly**. Suddenly, the **wheels** left the **ground** and I was **floating** above the road. The next minute I **found** myself at a great **height** above the **houses**. I could see **people** in their **gardens** and I could look down on birds **flying** below me!

The experience was **wonderful** and I have never felt **happier** in my whole life.

What could happen next in this story?

Teacher's notes

The three assessment texts on the following page can be used to sample pupils' progress, giving a 'snapshot' of their current level of competence in spelling. Most of the words appear in the sets of words that the pupils have been practising but others are introduced as they follow similar patterns to known words.

Assessment 1 features 25 words to spell. Multiplying each pupil's score by 4 will give a percentage result. Assessments 2 and 3 both have 20 words to spell. Multiplying by 5 will give a percentage result.

To administer each test, dictate the full passage before issuing the test sheets. Dictate the passage again very slowly, ensuring that each child is keeping up with your reading. Allow time for the children to write each of the missing words.

You could use the assessments on several occasions to track progress, using only one test on each occasion. Are there particular words or spelling patterns that cause difficulties for some children? If so, would the pupils benefit from revisiting the lists that feature these?

As an extra activity you could ask the pupils to extend each story. What happens next? How well can the children spell the words that they choose for their own part of the story?

 Andrew Brodie: Improving Spelling for Ages 8–9 © A&C Black, Bloomsbury Publishing 2011

Assessment 1

Name   Date

On my _____ my mum and I went for a walk _____ the
_____. We went past the _____ and the _____ then
_____ the _____ ground. We _____ for a while to
_____ the _____. When we realised that we _____
know how to play the game, we _____ and _____ on.

The path became _____ as it passed through lots of _____. It
became _____ again as we left the town _____. Now we were in
the countryside we _____ see for miles. There were some _____
riding _____ but they _____ a long way _____. They
_____ have been too far _____ because a couple of minutes later
I was quite _____ when they galloped past us.

Score   /25 =   %

Assessment 2

Name   Date

My sister is a _____ and she's _____ to me! She's _____
years old and I'm only nine so _____ I'm _____ she thinks she can
do _____ things and get away with them. One day I went into my
_____ and _____ that she had tied a _____ in every one of
my socks! I was so _____ that I took all her socks and hid them where
she _____ _____ find them – I put them _____ the sofa.

Later that day we were both _____ on the sofa _____ television.
I _____ the socks and began _____.

"What are you _____ about?" she _____.

"Nothing," I _____.

Score   /20 =   %

Assessment 3

Name   Date

When I was _____ I had a red _____ but now I have a blue _____. I like to think that my bike is quite _____ because when I'm on it I can fly. It's _____!

Yesterday I was _____ to see my _____. I was _____ late so I began pedalling really _____. Suddenly, the _____ left the _____ and I was _____ above the road. The next minute I _____ myself at a great _____ above the _____. I could see _____ in their _____ and I could look down on birds _____ below me!

The experience was _____ and I have never felt _____ in my whole life.

Score   /20 =   %